NI

D0103859

It is with a heart filled with love, appreciation, and gratitude that this book is dedicated to my most able assistant and dearest friend, Joan Gschwind.

Introduction

Proverbs have been called "the tears of humanity and the wisdom of the ages," "the fruit of the longest experience in the fewest words," or, as Cervantes phrased it, "a short sentence founded on long experience." These are indeed accurate descriptions of the proverbs of China. One will quickly find that beautifully and skillfully interwoven in Chinese proverbs is a philosophy which might be called "common-sense morality."

Four thousand years of Chinese history have provided us with an especially rich treasury of these pithy expressions of wisdom. From time immemorial shrewd observations of human relationships have been condensed in concise proverbs, and passed from generation to generation to serve as guiding principles in the lives of the Chinese people. To understand the ethics of the Chinese people and the philosophical background of their outlook on life, one can do no better than to study their proverbs.

Wisdom is one and universal, so it is not at all unusual to find an English equivalent or counterpart to a Chinese proverb. The delightful difference is in the picturesque wording. For example, in English we say, "Nothing ventured, nothing gained." In Chinese, it is paralleled by "If you do not scale the mountain, you cannot view the plain." In English we might say "Don't meet troubles halfway." The Chinese counterpart would be, "Wait till you come to the river before pulling off your shoes." Here the Chinese versions, though slightly longer, conjure up a more lively image, although brevity is generally essential to a good proverb and anything superfluous must be cut away.

The ancient philosophers of China favored simple, concise statements over complex ones, and some of the oldest Chinese proverbs are directly descended from these very philosophers.

One expects nothing less from an ancient culture populated with logical thinkers than a wealth of proverbs steeped in attractiveness and charm. And so, it is with great pride that this collection of some of the finest, most meaningful proverbs in all the world is presented. Read and enjoy.

—GUY A. ZONA

If You Have Two Loaves of Bread,

Sell One and Buy a Lily

Words are sounds of the heart.

Before everyone's door there is a part of heaven.

Nobody's family can hang up the sign, "Nothing the matter here."

Better an earth-lined cave from which the stars are visible than a golden pagoda roofed with iniquity.

If you don't wonder at the wonderful it ceases to be a wonder.

Slander is a daily occurrence, but if nobody listened, it would soon cease.

If you have nothing to do, go home early.

Although there exist many thousand subjects of elegant conversation, there are persons who cannot meet a cripple without talking about feet.

An unhappy person compares life to a shirt button, because it so often hangs by a thread.

If you would extend the fields of your happiness, the soil of your heart must be leveled.

If your strength will serve, go forward in the ranks; if not, stand still.

To know another is not to know that person's face, but to know that person's heart.

Whispered words are heard afar.

One cannot manage too many affairs; like pumpkins in the water, one pops up while you try to hold down the other.

If you have two loaves of bread, sell one and buy a lily.

The mind covers more ground than the heart, but goes less far.

Ice is not frozen three-feet thick with one day's cold.

Heaven and hell both have their quiet land.

A piece of paper blown by the wind into a court of law may in the end need to be drawn out again by two oxen.

He who grasps, loses.

The same faults which one condemns when out of office, one commits while in.

There is no fence that does not allow the wind through.

What is truly within will be manifested without.

The real fault is to have faults and not to amend them.

Though conversing face-to-face, hearts may have a thousand miles between them.

A person's heart seems never satisfied; the snake would swallow the elephant.

To go beyond is as bad as to fall short.

Better be the beak of a chicken than the rump of an ox.

If one branch does not move, none of the other branches will be swayed.

If a chattering bird be not placed in the mouth, vexation will not sit between the eyebrows.

One dog barks at nothing, the rest bark at him.

Entertain no thoughts which you would blush at in words.

The sweeter the perfume, the uglier the flies that gather around the bottle.

There are pictures to be seen in poems and poems that are seen in pictures.

Misfortune is not that which can be avoided but that which cannot.

Often the body may be healed but not the mind.

In the prosperity and decay of the state common folk have their share.

Pleasures were cheap before money became dear.

A raging wind strikes only those who are in it.

To say is easy; in trying to do, one finds many difficulties.

When one is past thirty, one can about half-comprehend the weather.

Whether we walk quickly or slowly, the road remains the same.

Purchased virtue is always much too dear.

Although the river is broad, there are times when boats collide.

There is no light burden on a long road.

The shadow moves as the sun directs.

The tongue is soft but constantly remains; the teeth are hard yet they fall out.

Wisdom is often nearer when we stoop than when we soar.

To do a kindness near home is better than going far away to burn incense.

Let the politeness of first acquaintance characterize all future meetings, then in the longest of friendships nothing disagreeable will arise.

If you use the heart with which you reprove others to reprove yourself, faults will lessen; if you use the heart with which you forgive yourself to forgive others, therein perfect friendship manifests.

To be entirely at leisure for one day is to be for one day immortal.

Those who go out of their house in search of happiness run after shadows.

We comb our hair every morning, why not our hearts?

When a finger points at the moon, the fool stares at the finger.

If a parent will not be a parent, a child should still be a child.

If you sin against heaven, there is no place for prayer.

Gods and angels also make blunders.

Under heaven nothing is impossible, all that is needed is a person with a pure heart.

Use heaven for your compass when your conscience is not at the helm.

It is the emptiness of our hearts that makes them spiritually receptive.

To praise someone every day adds to their happiness and long life.

Govern a family as you would cook a small fish—very gently.

.

However stupid some may be, they grow clever enough when chastising others; however wise, they may become a fool when chastising themselves.

Who considers everything decides nothing.

Drunkenness does not produce faults; it discovers them.

Those who take medicine and neglect their diet waste the skill of the physician.

Keep company with goodness and goodness will reflect.

The three secrets of happiness: See no evil, hear no evil, do no evil.

Happiness and misery are not fated but self-sought.

The best kind of acquaintance is acquaintance with each other's hearts.

Conduct yourself as if you were watching over an infant.

A truly great person never puts away the simplicity of a child.

There are many who say they are good, but who can tell the sex of a crow?

A person may be arrested by mistake, but not released.

To see a person's face is always better than hearing of their reputation.

If you set out on a journey of ten miles, remember that nine miles is only halfway.

Wine does not intoxicate men; men intoxicate themselves.

When a bird is about to die, its notes are mournful; when human beings are about to die, their words are good.

A dog has no aversion to a poor family.

One who can grasp opportunity as it slips by does not need a lucky dream.

The gods cannot help those who lose opportunities.

To read a book for the first time is to make the acquaintance of a new friend; to read it a second time is to meet an old one.

If heaven drops you a date, it must be received with an open mouth.

There is nothing impossible in this world; the only fear is that those of determination are wanting.

There are many paths to the top of the mountain, but the view always remains the same.

The one who removed the mountain was the one who began carrying away the small stones.

The wise forget insults as the ungrateful forget a kindness.

Fish see the bait but not the hook; we see the profit but not the peril.

A journey of a thousand miles begins with a single step.

It is better to light a candle than to curse the darkness.

Give a man a fish, and you feed him for a day. Teach a man to fish, and you feed him for a lifetime.

The path of duty lies in the thing that is nearby, but we seek it in that which is distant.

Relations must be seldom visited; kitchens and gardens often.

For a kindness as small as a drop of water, one should give in return a whole spring.

Each interprets in his own way the music of heaven.

The dog in the kennel barks at its fleas; the dog that hunts does not feel them.

Power has no friends, envy has no rest, and crime has no satisfaction.

The great never feel great; the small never feel small.

It is not the horse that costs money, it is the saddle.

Medicine cures curable sickness.

A good horse is to be ridden.

An honest magistrate has lean clerks; a powerful god has fat priests.

It costs no strength to watch others labor.

It's no use starving the horse to fatten the mule.

The wise hen is never too old to dread springtime.

Do the lame offer to carry the footsore; the blind to protect the one-eyed?

Lending is like throwing away; receiving payment is like finding something.

A chance day is better than a chosen day.

The time and the place and the loved one are never all together.

In difficulties we are easily tested and easily saved.

If there is a custom, do not seek to diminish it; if there is no custom, do not seek to add one.

When the flight is not high, the fall is not hard.

All people have faces as all trees have bark.

Once the fire is lighted, it cannot be commanded by anyone as to what it will burn and what it will leave untouched.

Who has children cannot long remain poor; who has none cannot long remain rich.

A kind word warms for three winters.

Gold sinks deeper than dross.

Without error, there can be no such thing as truth.

Present to the eye, present to the mind.

What the eye does not see, the heart does not grieve for.

Everything can be gotten or obtained by politeness.

A three years' drought will not starve a cook.

Half a lifetime's fame provokes the resentment of a hundred generations.

Being polite means taking nothing amiss.

Do not forget little kindnesses, and do not remember small faults.

Trees are for shade and children are for old age.

No one blames you for being too polite.

Hearing is paradise, and seeing is hell.

Possessed of happiness? Do not exhaust it.

Blessings come not in pairs; misfortunes come not singly.

Though you have much gold you cannot buy that which is not for sale.

Bald-headed men are ready-made Buddhist priests.

Where no money is spent, no grace is gained.

Spending money is like water soaking into sand.

A good heart always does a little extra.

Any soil will do to bury in.

In China, there are more tutors than scholars and more physicians than patients.

Kindness is more binding than a loan.

A bully does not owe debts.

Only inferiors flatter superiors.

Affect a little indistinctness rather than insist upon absolute correct-
ness.

When joy is extreme, it is the forerunner of grief.

When we retreat and ponder a matter, everything appears more difficult.

In truthful revealing it is not necessary to prepare a preliminary draft.

Even genii sometimes drop their swords.

Listen to all, pluck a feather from every passing goose, but follow no one absolutely.

In good works do not yield to others.

When children go abroad, they take with them their parents' knitting.

You can't chop a thing as round as you can pare it.

Every family has a goddess of mercy, every place has Amita Buddha.

Be inwardly clever but outwardly clownish.

Conceited people possess an odor.

There is a reward for good and a punishment for evil.

A child but a foot long requires three feet of cloth.

A thousand or ten-thousand reckonings of mankind are not equal to one reckoning of heaven.

Beware of helping yourself to corn from the manger of a blind mule.

If you are charitable you cannot become rich; if you are rich you cannot be charitable.

The flower attracts the bee, but when it departs, it is to the bee's lips that the honey clings.

A bow long bent waxes weak.

Books speak to the mind, friends to the heart, heaven to the soul, all else to the ears.

The good bee will not sip from a faded flower.

The heart of a little child is like the heart of Buddha.

God will never slight sorrowful people.

Stand and borrow, kneel and beg the return.

The competent execute, the incompetent enjoy the advantage.

Men and beasts are all alike.

The sea of Buddha has no shore.

Those who have not tasted the bitterest of life's bitters can never appreciate the sweetest of life's sweets.

The hand that feeds the ox grasps the knife when it is fattened.

The foot of the lamp is the worst lighted.

The lightning discovers objects which the paper lantern fails to reveal.

When the lips are gone the teeth are cold.

God responds to us as quickly as shadow to form or echo to voice.

The gem of the sky is the sun; the gem of the house is the child.

Small pairs of trousers never come singly.

After a typhoon there are pears to gather.

Steal needles when young and you'll steal money when old.

In beating a dog have regard to its master.

Doctors knock at no doors; they only come when invited.

Dogs have more good in them than people think they have.

To take no medicine is as good as a middling doctor.

If you pray to Buddha, pray to only one.

Water always flows downhill.

If one wishes to be acquainted with the past and the present, five cart-loads of books must be read

Cold water entering the mouth drops into the heart.

Haste comes of the evil one, leisure from God.

Oblige and you will be obliged.

Reason will not act in vain.

You can reflect what is another's; you can take satisfaction only in what is your own.

A thousand remembrances do not give one thought.

Walls have ears.

To have money is to add on thirty years' dignity.

In every small foot there is a jar full of tears.

Books do not exhaust words, nor words thoughts.

When the wild bird lacks food, all the earth is before him.

A family that has an old person in it has a jewel.

Losing comes of winning money.

The one-legged never stumble.

When your mouth eats, let it consult with your stomach.

If the flower is good, the fruit will be good.

Parents are never in the wrong.

Turn in before nightfall, and arise at cockcrow.

49

With money you can move the gods; without it you cannot move people.

The fear of death is the beginning of discipline.

Humans' arithmetic is small; heaven deals in large figures.

Birth and death are decreed; wealth and honor rest with God.

None will carry on a money-losing business, but some will engage in a head-losing occupation.

You can't be the head of a family unless you show yourself both stupid and deaf.

When the canals are full, the wells are full.

The body is born whole by the mother; it is for the son to return it again whole.

Everything in the past died yesterday; everything in the future was born today.

The money-maker is never weary; the weary man never makes money.

The fairest morrow does not restore yesterday.

To obtain one leads to wishing for two.

Without the past, we never could have had the present.

Rain and dew are mercies; so are ice and frost.

A fair wind raises no storm.

To look at a plum is not to quench one's thirst.

Pretense may become reality.

It doesn't matter whether you are right or not, if you have no money you are wrong.

T'ien (God) is three feet over your head.

The wind has the wind goddess to govern it.

When it is dark the sun no longer shines, but who shall forget the colors of the rainbow?

Rain in spring is as precious as oil.

Everybody is obliged to help rascals and orphans.

The pleasure of doing good is the only pleasure which will not wear out.

Unfading are the gardens of kindness.

Politeness costs nothing and gains everything.

A lame cat is better than a swift horse when rats infest the palace.

A boy is born facing in; a girl is born facing out.

The people's heart is heaven's will.

If one has plenty of money but no child, one cannot be reckoned rich; if one has children but no money, one cannot be considered poor.

The competent toil, the incompetent rest.

Rotten wood cannot be carved, and mud walls cannot be plastered.

A dry finger cannot pick up salt.

The wise are great in small things; the vicious small in great things.

Raise your sail one foot and you get ten feet of wind.

For one word we are often deemed wise; for one word we are often deemed foolish.

Don't raise waves in the world and you'll keep ice and cold out of your bosom.

Bitter words are medicine; sweet words an epidemic.

Buddha lives in one's heart.

Concealing truth is like wearing embroidered clothes and traveling by night.

From life to death is one's reach.

Who gives bad wine to his guests will only drink tea in their houses.

To the desert traveler all wells are sparkling.

The whip that's lost always has a golden handle.

All the rivers run into the sea, yet the sea is not full.

It is easy to avoid a naked spear but not a hidden sword.

Truth often hides in an ugly pool.

Though you don't believe in other gods, you believe in the God of Thunder; though you don't believe in medicine generally, you believe in laxatives.

There is no seed to greatness.

One sees short; two see long.

One "see" is worth a hundred "tells."

Little with patience will grow to much.

It is easier to obtain thousands of gold pieces than kind words.

The host is happy when the guest is gone.

Flattering a man of wisdom is like adding flowers to embroidery.

The sea is not worn by ships, nor is a road ruined by travel.

When there are no fish in the river, shrimp are valued.

In China, we have only three religions, but we have a hundred dishes we can make from rice.

Ten tacls will move the gods; one hundred will move heaven itself.

The tongue weaves for clothes; the pen tills for food.

When one wants a thing long enough, eventually one won't.

In plenty, think of want; in want, do not presume on plenty.

The chance-planted willow twig grows into a shade tree.

We are no more virtuous without exhortation than does a bell sound without being struck.

Marriage, wealth, children, and pay are all predestined.

Without money, it is no use calling—no one will come.

While traveling, do not reckon the distance; while eating, do not reckon the quantity.

Which of these are first broken? The tired truce, the vulture's fast, or the Moi's promise.

No ease for the mouth when one tooth is aching.

The lame duck should avoid the ploughed field.

Sitting with your back to a draft is the same as looking straight into your coffin.

Dogs will love and admire the meanest of us and feed our colossal vanity with their uncritical homage.

The great river does not reject the small streams.

The softest things in the world override the hardest.

What is said to a person's face is not slander.

If something is done for you, it must always be regarded as good.

Much courtesy forestalls offense.

Murder may be condoned, but discourtesy never.

When the sun sets, the moon rises; when the moon sets, the sun rises.

One acrid taste relieves three longings of the stomach.

Kindness to the starfish is as wind in the desert.

A man may tell what he has seen.

When a road is uneven, those who are on each side level it.

Discretion is the handmaiden of truth.

Hospitality is the virtue of children and the wisdom of the ancestor.

He who confounds morals must confound manners.

Charity is not a bone you throw to a dog, but a bone you share with a dog.

If you love your children, give them plenty of cudgel; if you hate them, cram them with dainties.

If at home you receive no visitors, when abroad you will have no host.

A tree blown down by the wind has more branches than roots.

Who speaks within walls is listened to outside.

It is a homely face that comforts and a coarse cloth that warms.

The very word *forbearance* is precious in a house.

The hearts that are the nearest are those that touch.

One may give up a father though he be a magistrate, but not a mother though she be a beggar.

Without money do not enter a crowd; in adversity do not seek your relatives.

Take no notice of what you hear said on the pillow.

There is no ladle that never strikes the edge of the cooking pot.

A year's opportunities depend on the spring; a day's on the dawn; a family's on harmony; and a life's on industry.

Nowadays, eyelids are thin.

It is the sick duck that is worried by the weasel.

If you do not pay the doctor who has cured you, beware of falling ill again.

Who knows not how to boast knows not how to succeed.

Keep your broken arm inside your sleeve.

All human affairs are my affairs.

All bad flesh smells alike.

No grief so great as a dead heart.

Unpolished jade is not a gem.

One key doesn't rattle.

One day husband and wife implies a hundred days' kindness.

Conquer a dog before you contend with a lion.

If the domestic duties be duly performed, where is the necessity of going afar to burn incense?

To a bachelor of arts, kindness is but half a sheet of paper.

Bad descendants involve ancestors in disgrace.

Though the left hand conquer the right, no advantage is gained.

If you wish your children to have a quiet life, let them always be a little hungry and cold.

Teach your descendants the two proper roads—literature and farming.

When brothers work together, mountains are turned into gold.

The front boat is eyes for the boat behind.

It is the beautiful bird that gets caged.

In bed—husband and wife, out of bed—guests.

Better meals without meat than a home without harmony.

One dog looks at something, and a hundred dogs look at him.

We never wander so far as when we think we know the way.

Crows are black all the world over.

The culprit talks small when he sees the bamboo.

When you are very angry, don't go to law; when you are very hungry, don't make verses.

Whether you meet men or devils, talk as they do.

Those who speak well have not always the best things.

The mark must be made in youth.

When the oil is exhausted, the lamp goes out.

Old ginger is the sharpest.

When the arrow is on the string, it must go.

Fine words are incredible; credible words are not fine.

The tree exists for its fruit; humans for righteousness and self-control.

Every sect has its doctrine and every doctrine its sect.

If what we see is doubtful, how can we believe what is spoken behind the back?

To see a man do a good deed is to forget all his other faults.

Better establish a branch than cut off a line.

The cabbage grub in the end dies in the cabbage.

Enlightened people perform no dark deeds.

It is a mark of insincerity of purpose to spend one's time in looking for the sacred emperor in the low-class tea shops.

Our convenience is the convenience of others.

Feast, and your halls are crowded; fast, and the world goes by.

To plan affairs rests with us; to complete affairs rests with heaven.

A host who escorts a guest no farther than the door is not a real host.

Those who know how to do a thing do not find it difficult; those who find it difficult know not how to do it.

If one has resolution one can live by it, if not, one must live by the toil of one's hands.

A good conscience always pays well.

We are evaluated by our clothes, a horse by its saddle.

Who sends charcoal in a snowstorm is the true superior.

There are three-hundred rules of ceremony and three-thousand rules of behavior.

Destroy all passion while you light Buddha's lamp.

If you bow at all, bow low.

Draw your bow, but do not discharge the arrow; it is better to frighten than to strike.

A hunting dog will at last die a violent death.

To hand over the bow is to hand over the arrow.

That from which we can escape is not an ill.

Deal with evil as if it were a sickness in your person.

The best cure for drunkenness is to see a drunken man while you are sober.

The most securely shut door is the one that could be left open.

They who know their hearts mistrust their eyes.

Three-tenths of good looks are due to nature; seven-tenths to dress.

Never be boastful; someone may come along who knew you as a child.

What one hears by gossip is empty; what one beholds with the eye is solid.

When people are friendly even water is sweet.

Gold is tested by fire, people by gold.

He who knows he is a fool is not a big fool.

One has never so much need of one's wit as when dealing with a fool.

An immoderate use of dainties generally ends in disease; pleasure when past is converted into pain.

When aroused, become awake; when awake, reach understanding.

Fools never admire themselves so much as when they have committed some folly.

Thinking of others' advantage will turn out to one's own.

When one is angry one cannot be in the right.

A beast's spots are on the outside; human spots are on the inside.

Behave toward everyone as if receiving a great guest.

The first part of the night, think of your own faults; the latter, think of the faults of others.

Who does not believe in others finds others do not believe in them.

Heaven has a road, but no one travels it; Hell has no gate, but we bore through to get there.

It is easier to slip from frugality to extravagance then to pass from extravagance to frugality.

Do not eat the fruit of the stricken branch.

The error of one moment becomes the sorrow of a lifetime.

When one falls, it is not one's foot that is to blame.

To carry out a fast is from within; to break a fast is from without.

The saddest dog sometimes wags its tail.

When you lift your hand to strike, you are three-tenths lower than your opponent.

Only fools seek credit from the achievements of their ancestors.

Newborn calves don't fear tigers.

Foolhardiness is as driving a fairy chariot on a long journey.

The most important thing in life is to get buried well.

Whoever can endure in poverty will keep his position when wealthy.

Where no money goes before, no road is open.

Money is hundred-footed.

Only after many days can one's heart be seen.

Even a bad coin must have two sides.

If they are not of your sort, they should not enter your door.

Doctor your teeth as you govern the military—with severity; doctor your eyes as you govern the people—with gentleness.

If the dog goes when the cat comes, there will be no quarreling.

Let the dead care for the dead and the living for the living.

When we come face-to-face, our differences vanish.

A dog is not the only creature that barks.

There is always a way to open any door.

A boat straightens its course when it gets to a bridge.

In opening a book there is always profit.

You can't swallow dates whole.

If a man is a miser he will certainly have a prodigal son.

Stable in poverty, stable in mind.

Who tells me of my faults is my teacher; who tells me of my virtues does me harm.

Deal with the faults of others as gently as with your own.

Ask no favors and people everywhere are affable; if you don't drink, it doesn't matter what price wine is.

Always leave some way of escape for the erring.

A red-nosed may be a teetotaller, but no one will believe it.

Towers are measured by their shadows, great people by their kharma.

Those who know do not speak; those who speak do not know.

Those who speak well have not always the best things.

Beware of silent dogs and silent water.

There is always a rogue to rob a rogue.

Use people as you would use wood; because one inch is worm-eaten, you would never throw away the whole trunk.

When you are with the wolf, you must howl like the wolves.

Most trees are more upright than most people.

A good question is like one beating a bell.

Cherish the false prophet who predicts disaster and the true one who foresees health.

The pure upon seeing it pure, call it pure.

If one word misses the mark, a thousand will do the same.

A healthy poor person is half a rich one.

If two keep a horse, it is thin; if two families keep a boat, it leaks.

First impressions rule the mind.

If you owe a person anything, there is nothing like seeing them often.

Life springs from sorrow and calamity, and death from ease and pleasures.

An inch of gold cannot buy an inch of time.

If you wish to succeed, consult three old people.

The mountains of today are not so lofty as the mountains of yore.

One casts a net of golden meshes with both hands and draws in a hundred misfortunes.

Though a tree be a thousand chang in height, its leaves must return to the earth at last.

Don't think to hunt two hares with one dog.

Poverty and an ugly face cannot be hid.

Who lacks a single tael sees many bargains.

The poorer one is, the more devils one meets.

The dragon in shallow water becomes the butt of shrimps.

Money makes the blind see and the priest sell his holy books.

One needn't devour a whole chicken to know the flavor of the bird.

The young won't make efforts and the old make them in vain.

To believe in one's dreams is to spend all one's life asleep.

Without sorrow none can become a saint.

When good fortune is exhausted, evil fortune follows.

There is sure to be fuel near a big tree.

No needle is sharp at both ends.

If the string is long, the kite will fly high.

In years of plenty, jade; in lean years, grain.

If there be no light in the east, there will be in the west.

When lucky times come, flowers will be added to the embroidery.

Milk, by repeated agitation, turns to butter.

Light words are easily spoken behind barred doors.

To those who wait, time opens every door.

There is often a space between the fish and the fish plate.

The trotting horse hears not the storyteller's yarn.

Serve but a day and you are a slave; carry four ounces of silver on the shoulder and you are a merchant.

You must have a couple of grains of rice in order to catch fowls.

In misfortune, gold is dull; in happiness, iron is bright.

The lotus springs from the mud.

Cease to struggle and you cease to live.

There is mutual love between those of the same creed; mutual jealousy between those of the same trade.

Done leisurely, done well.

The palest ink is better than the most retentive memory.

Who sews hemp will reap hemp; who sows beans will reap beans.

If you never go up a hill, you will never know what a plain is like.

The less indulgence one has for oneself, the more one may have for others.

If jade is not polished, it cannot become a thing of use.

Swiftly running water is a good place to catch fish.

Customers are to be valued; goods are mere grass.

If you would not be cheated, ask the price at three shops.

If you suspect someone, don't employ them; if you employ someone, don't suspect them.

Be the first to the field and the last to the couch.

Poor by condition, rich by ambition.

Cats purr in thankfulness when God tells them they are good cats.

A bachelor of arts discusses books; a pork butcher, pigs.

One is happy when one has books, but happier still when one has no need of them.

Able to buy, don't so buy as to frighten the seller; able to sell, don't so sell as to frighten the buyer.

Without resolution we must make our living by the sweat of our brow.

Who toils with pain will eat with pleasure.

A joy that's shared is a joy made double.

Before you think of buying, calculate on selling.

The great wall stands; the builder is gone.

Great people never feel great; small people never feel small.

When cat meets cat they kiss in kindness.

The greater your troubles, the greater is your opportunity to show your-self a worthy person.

For a gentleman there is no other name; he is always a gentleman.

With patience the mulberry leaf becomes a silk gown.

They who would rise in the world should veil their ambition with humility.

Better be small and shine than be great and cast a great shadow.

Just scales and full measures cause no one harm.

Deal with evil as if it were a sickness within yourself.

Truth is truth, though spoken by an enemy.

A candle as big as a cup cannot illuminate tomorrow.

When the leading carriage is upset the next one is more careful.

Carrying poles which bend easily do not break.

When a cat and a rat sleep together, death is well in sight.

The more you eat, the less flavor; the less you eat, the more flavor.

Other people's donkeys turn the mill best; a priest from a distant place best reads the ritual.

At court, one sings to drink; at the inn, one drinks to sing.

A door has two gods, one good, the other severe.

Modesty has more charm than beauty.

Condemn the sin, not the sinner.

A good intention clothes itself with sudden power.

The end of passion is the beginning of repentance.

To know one's self is to know others, for heart can understand heart.

There are a thousand miseries in one falling in love.

Rare and far between visits increase love.

Who knows two languages has double worth.

Good companionship protects from evil.

The seducer is brother to the murderer, and silence the sister of complaisance.

Patience reaps peace, and rashness regret; the former riches, the latter poverty.

Who loves life must practice meekness.

Sin and happiness cannot dwell together.

Fine words and an insinuating appearance are seldom associated with true virtue.

Learn as though you would never be able to master it. Hold it as though you would be in fear of losing it.

If I am virtuous and worthy, for whom should I not maintain a proper concern?

There are two innocent men: one dead, the other unborn.

A young branch takes on all the bends that one gives it.

Who would rise in the world should veil ambition with the priorities of humanity.

A bird cannot roost but on one branch. A mouse can drink no more than its fill from a river.

Happiness is like a sunbeam, which the least shadow intercepts.

The loftiest towers rise from the ground.

Procrastination is the thief of time.

What needs no display is virtue.

How seldom in life is the moon overhead.

Truly polite is always polite.

Without feelings of respect, what is there to distinguish us from beasts?

There is not a better counselor than a competitor for the overthrow of an enemy.

Blame yourself as you would blame others; excuse others as you would yourself.

When you drink from the stream remember the spring.

If a superior person abandons virtue, how can the requirements of that name be fulfilled?

Many boats do not obstruct a channel; many vehicles do not block the road.

We do not calculate when the blossom is out.

Credit cuts off customers.

There are customers for all sorts of goods.

Great oaks from little acorns grow.

He who would govern others must first govern himself.

Better to fail in a high aim than to succeed in a low one.

If the son of heaven breaks the law, he is guilty like one of the people.

Learn the past and you will know the future.

Riches adorn only the house; virtue adorns the person.

Attention to small things is the economy of virtue.

Those who labor with their minds rule; those who labor with their bodies are ruled.

What the superior man seeks in himself, the small man seeks in others.

Thought unassisted by learning is perilous.

Silence is a true friend that never betrays.

To see the right and not to do it is cowardice or lack of principle.

It is only he who possesses absolute truth in the world who can create.

Leisure breeds lust.

The good-looking woman needs no paint.

Never quarrel with a woman.

In the boy see the man.

Better prevent than cure disease.

It is sincerity that places a crown upon our lives.

Goodness does not consist in greatness, but greatness in goodness.

Wine is the discoverer of secrets.

A cautious tongue insures prosperity; adherence to industry averts want.

Kindness to a puppy is always repaid.

Ceremony is the smoke of friendship.

To forget one's ancestors is to be a brook without a source, a tree without a root.

Fuel is not sold in a forest, nor fish on a lake.

People of principle are sure to be bold, but those who are bold may not always be those of principle.

Experience is a comb that nature gives us when we are bald.

Who teaches me for a day is my father for a lifetime.

When one family has a lawsuit, ten families are involved.

The most priceless treasure of all is extensive reading.

Of all important things, the first is not to cheat conscience.

Do good regardless of consequences.

Matters are more easily discussed than accomplished.

Out of the wolf's den, into the tiger's mouth.

We require God's help even in moving one inch.

Husbandry and letters are the two chief professions.

Scholars are their country's treasure, and the richest ornaments of the feast.

Where the prince leads, the people follow.

Practice becomes second nature.

The competent execute, the incompetent enjoy the advantage.

All pursuits are lean in comparison with learning.

Easy to learn, hard to master.

Thought without study is vain speculation; study without thought is mere words without knowledge.

Reading makes us full; contemplation, wise; and practice, perfect.

What we see and hear, heaven also sees and hears.

Who believes in gambling will one day sell his house.

Tigers and deer do not stroll together.

The prodigal's repentance is a priceless treasure.

In a united family happiness springs up of itself.

Fears are minimal where kinsmen and neighbors share sincerity.

Man cannot reach perfection in a hundred years.

Lambs have the grace to suck kneeling.

Would you know politics, read history.

The emperor is the father of his people, not a master to be served by slaves.

Killing a bad monarch is not to be considered murder but justice.

The wife of one cannot eat the rice of two.

If they match by nature then indeed they should marry.

Never do what you wouldn't have known.

As the promise, such should be the payment.

No matter the price, honor thy promise.

Putting on clothes, remember the weaver's work; eating daily food, remember the farmer's toil.

Guide the blind over the bridge and the lame over the threshold.

Nothing must divide the married pair, only death.

A guilty emperor will exhaust the mandates of heaven.

Win your lawsuit, lose your money.

The pen conveys one's meaning a thousand miles.

Schools hide future premieres.

Does the swallow know the wild goose's course?

Plants surpass men in recognizing spring.

Who will not work shall not eat.

Every family has a Goddess of Mercy.

In the husband, fidelity; in the wife, obedience.

The cleverest doctor cannot doctor himself.

Getting a thousand prescriptions is easy; obtaining a single cure is difficult.

Spilt water cannot be gathered up.

Strike while the iron is hot.

Mind is the lord of man.

Virtuous men are the emperor's treasure.

Naked we enter this world and naked we must leave.

Look not on temptation, and your mind will be at rest.

Better die than turn your back on reason.

It is a little thing to starve to death; it is a serious matter to lose one's virtue.

Better master of one than jack of all trades.

Injure others, injure yourself.

One generation plants the trees; another sits in their shade.

Unskilled workers become fools when they quarrel with their tools.

Everyone rakes the embers to his own cake.

An hour's blessing is worth a year's labor.

There are no two together but God makes a third.

Cast thy bread upon the waters; God will know of it if the fishes do not.

Time flies like an arrow; days and months like a shuttle.

Do not neglect your own in order to weed another's field.

The less indulgence one has for oneself, the more one may have for others.

Who goes out of their home in search of happiness runs after shadows.

He who knows his heart mistrusts his eyes.

Enlightened men pronounce sentence on themselves.

That from which we can escape is not an ill.

Everything is emptiness, and emptiness is everything.

False humility is genuine arrogance.

However stupid a man may be, he grows clever enough when blaming others; however wise, he becomes a fool when blaming himself.

He is wise who knows the truth when he hears it, and hearing, gives heed.

It is just as bad to take offense as to give offense.

Learning is fine clothes for the rich man, and riches for the poor man.

If custom is not indulged with custom, custom will weep.

Don't tell me what I was, but tell me what I am.

When one poor man assists another poor man, God himself laughs.